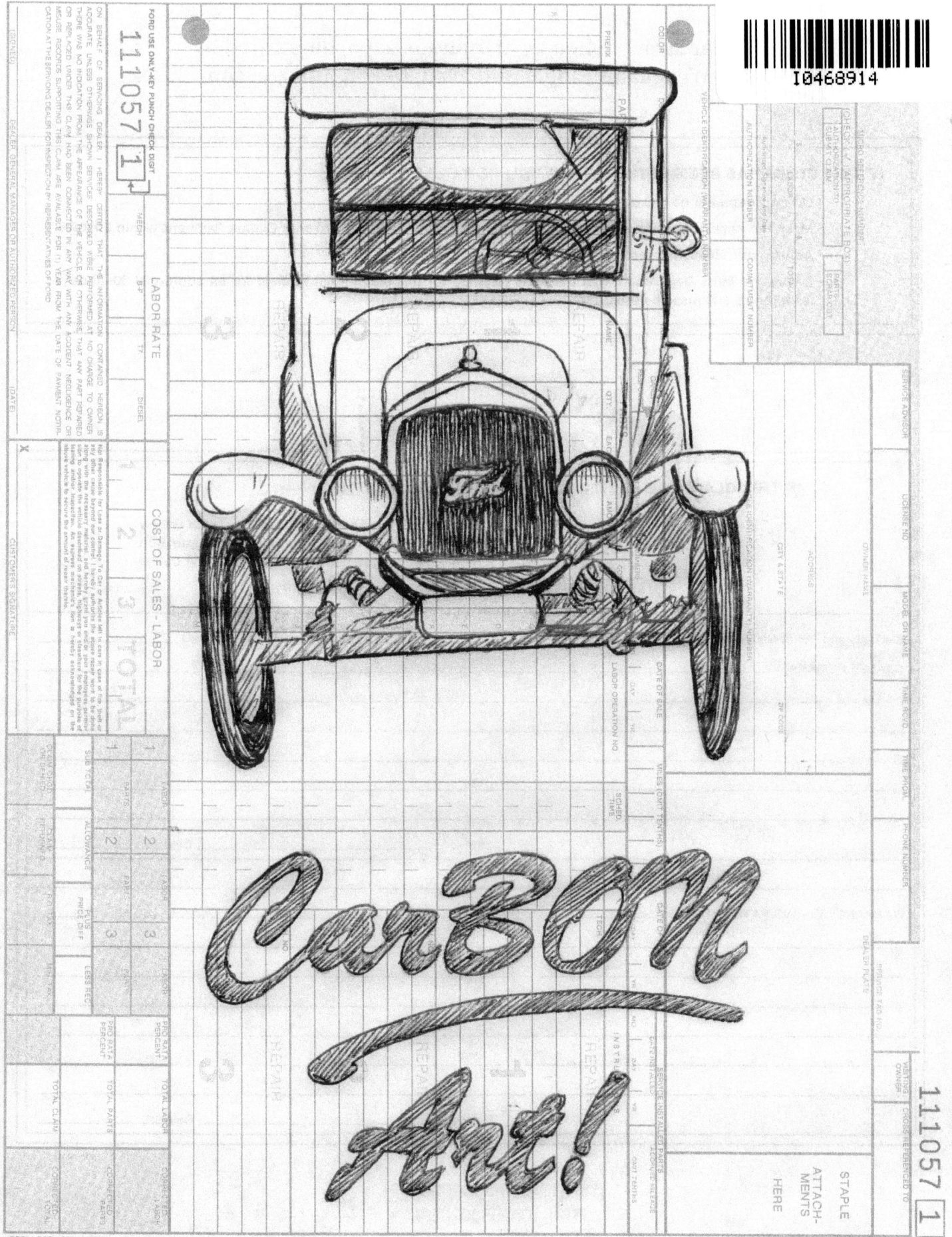

CarBON Art!

Copyright © 2016 by Art & Photos, LLC
www.artnphotos.com
ISBN-13: 978-1530028689
ISBN-10: 153002868X

Dedication

To my best friend and husband John who inspires me to accomplish things that I never thought possible.

Prologue

Years ago a friend of mine who used to own a car dealership gave me a box of carbon forms that were obsolete. I love carbon paper and use it for all kinds of projects, so I gladly accepted them. Each form had so many layers of carbon that I barely made a dent in the supply.

Fast forward twenty years and yes, I still have the box of forms. I am always looking to repurpose things and I happened to see drawings that someone had done on old ledger paper. It made me think of that box of really old serial-numbered carbon forms that I happened to possess. I drew a picture on one of them. How fun! I had three carbon copies to play with! My husband suggested that I draw old Ford cars because, after all, they were from an old Ford dealership.

So began my journey of drawing old Fords. I have never really looked at cars. If someone asked me to describe one I would say , "It was red or blue, or whatever color." I asked my friends and family what their favorite cars were to get an idea of what to draw. My mom learned to drive on a Model T Ford. She says it was an antique car in her day and she was a teenager, so that's what I started with. I gained a whole new appreciation for vehicles that I never had before. The lines, contours and details were fascinating! Suddenly, I was checking out cars everywhere I went. I even did a cell phone *paparazzi* on a cool old truck in a parking lot! I went to a car show and sold prints of my artwork and talked to other car lovers. I love to color and realized this might be something other people might like to do, too!

And now you know the rest of the story . . . .

111054 9

CROWN Victoria

1956

FORM FCS 1663 (11-80)   THE REYNOLDS & REYNOLDS CO., CELINA, OHIO   LITHO IN U.S.A.

FORD USE ONLY-KEY PUNCH CHECK DIGIT

STAPLE ATTACH-MENTS HERE

SERVICE ADVISOR

LICENSE NO.

OWNER NAME

MODEL OR NAME

PHONE NUMBER

TIME RCV'D.

TIME PROM.

DEALER PLATE

SERVICE TAG NO.

VISITING OWNER

CROSS REFERENCED TO

VEHICLE IDENTIFICATION (WARRANTY) NUMBER

CITY & STATE

PROGRAM CODE

AUTHORIZATION NUMBER

COMMITMENT NUMBER

CHECK (✓) APPROPRIATE BOX

PART NUMBERS

PREFIX   BASIC

COLOR   TRIM   PROD. DATE

DATE OF REPAIR

INSTRUCTIONS

PARTS

COST OF SALES - LABOR

1   2   3   TOTAL

LABOR RATE

MECH.   B-P   TY   DIESEL

TOTAL LABOR

TOTAL PARTS

PRO RATA PERCENT

CORRECTED LABOR

CORRECTED PARTS

TOTAL

FORD USE ONLY-KEY PUNCH CHECK DIGIT

111054 9

X

CUSTOMER'S SIGNATURE

(DATE)

DEALER GENERAL MANAGER OR AUTHORIZED PERSON

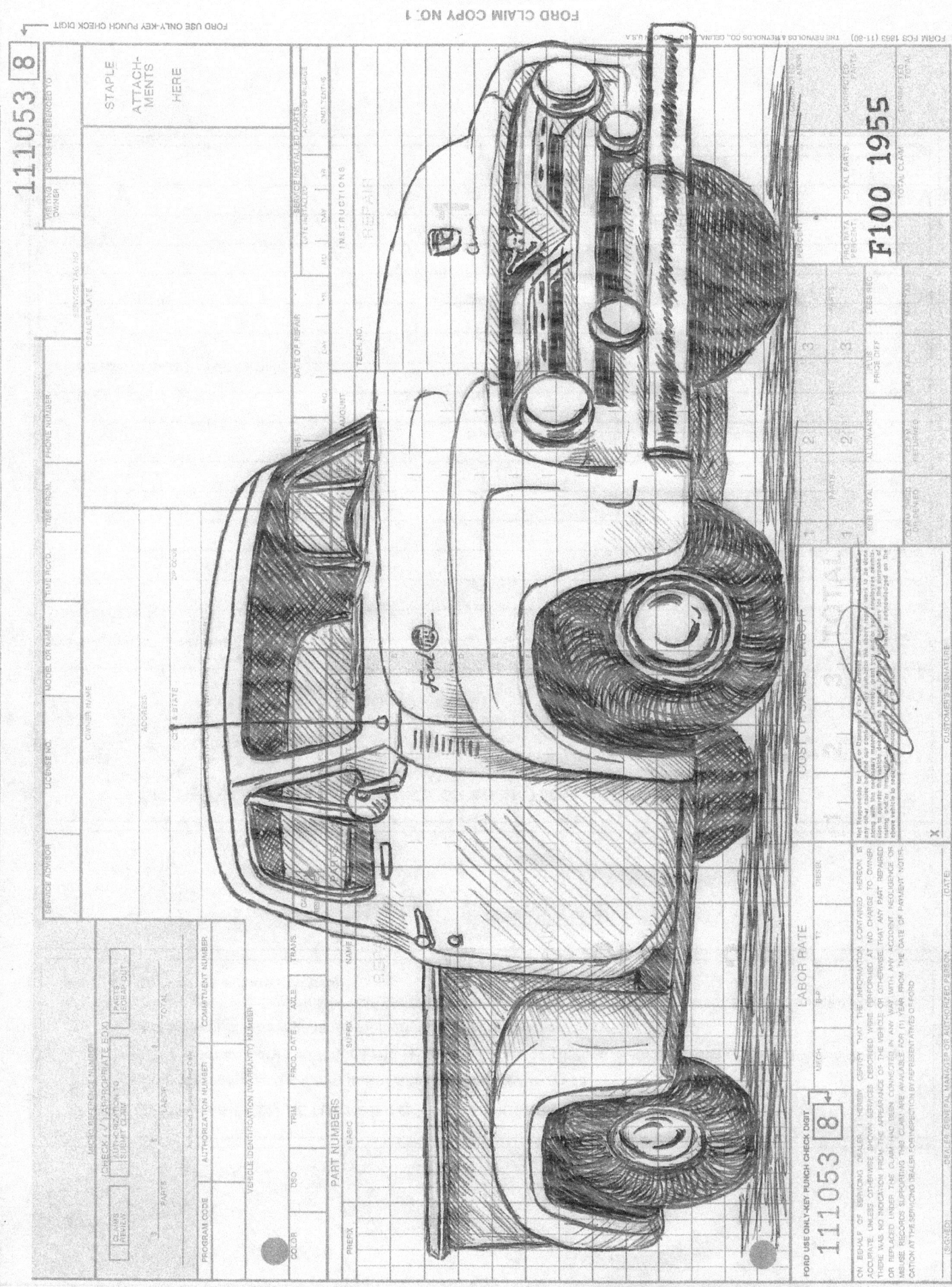

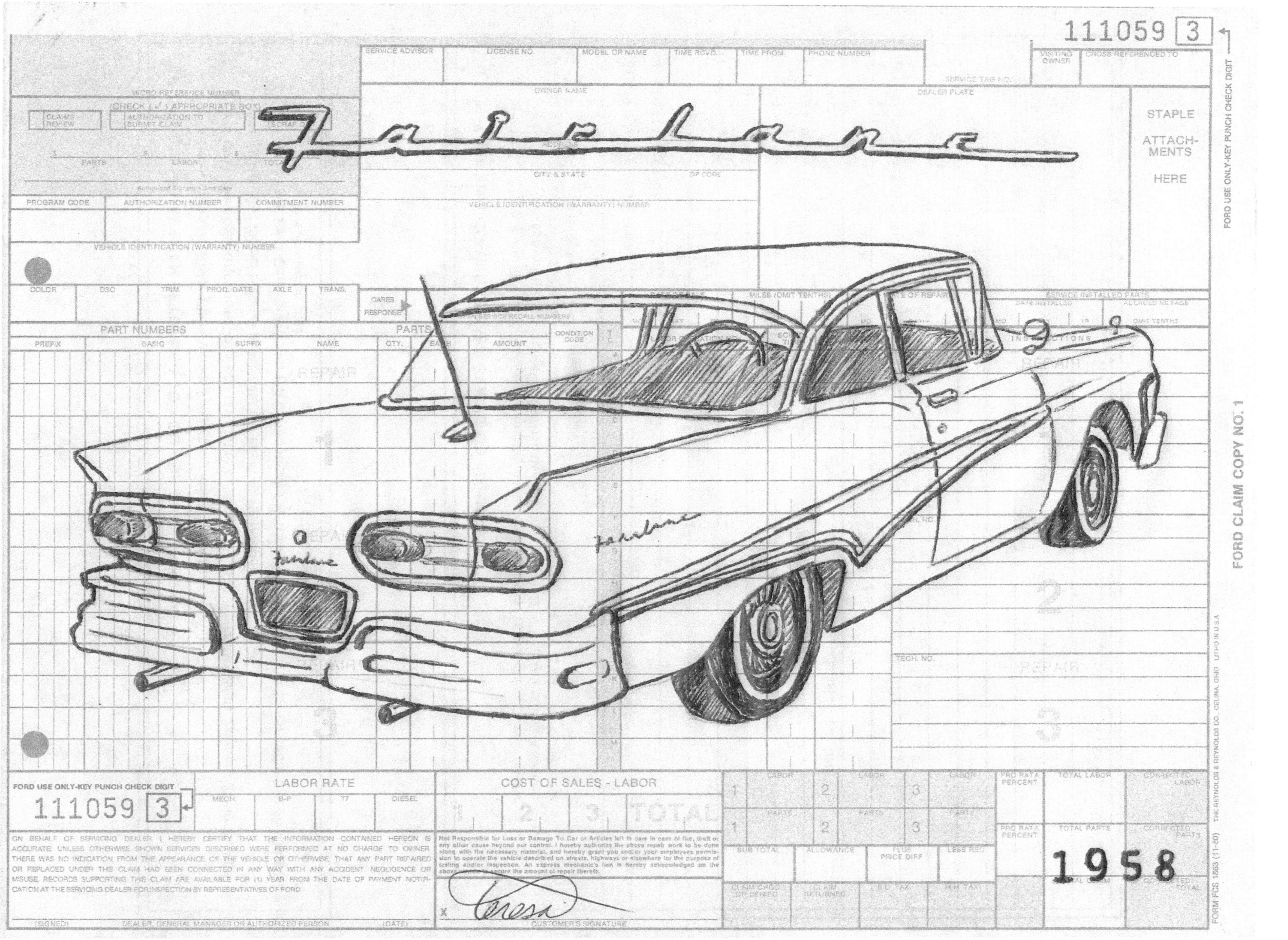
111059 3
Fairlane
STAPLE ATTACH-MENTS HERE
FORD CLAIM COPY NO. 1
FORD USE ONLY-KEY PUNCH CHECK DIGIT
111059 3
LABOR RATE
COST OF SALES - LABOR
1958

THE REYNOLDS & REYNOLDS CO., CELINA, OHIO   LITHO IN U.S.A.

FORM FCS 1865 (11-60)

111034 0

FORD USE ONLY-KEY PUNCH CHECK DIGIT

CROSS REFERENCED TO

STAPLE ATTACH-MENTS HERE

VISITING OWNER

DEALER PLATE

SERVICE TAG NO.

SERVICE ADVISOR

OWNER NAME

LICENSE NO.

MODEL OR NAME

PHONE NUMBER

TIME PROM.

TIME RCVD.

ADDRESS

CITY & STATE

ZIP CODE

VEHICLE IDENTIFICATION (WARRANTY) NUMBER

VEHICLE IDENTIFICATION (WARRANTY) NUMBER

AUTHORIZATION NUMBER

COMMITMENT NUMBER

PROGRAM CODE

CHECK (√) AS APPROPRIATE BOX:
AUTHORITY TO SUBMIT CLAIM   PARTS/SCRAP-OUT

COLOR   TRIM   ENG   PROD. DATE   AXLE   TRANS

PREFIX   BASIC   SUFFIX

PART NUMBERS

NAME

PARTS

CARS RESPONSE

DATE OF SALE   DATE OF REPAIR

MILES (OMIT TENTHS)

SCHED. TIME

AMOUNT

LABOR OPERATION NO.

TECH. NO.

SERVICE INSTALLED PARTS

INSTRUCTIONS

Galaxie
500

1963

TOTAL LABOR

TOTAL PARTS

TOTAL CLAIM

PRO RATA PERCENT

PRO RATA PERCENT

COST OF SALES - LABOR

LABOR RATE

MECH.   B-P   DIESEL

1   2   3   TOTAL

SUB TOTAL   ALLOWANCE   PRICE DIFF.   LESS REC.

CLAIMED OR OWED

CUSTOMER'S SIGNATURE

DEALER GENERAL MANAGER OR AUTHORIZED PERSON

(SIGNED)   (DATE)

FORD USE ONLY-KEY PUNCH CHECK DIGIT

111034 0

111063 | 7

FORD USE ONLY-KEY PUNCH CHECK DIGIT

STAPLE ATTACHMENTS HERE

Model A

Ford

1928

REPAIR

INSTRUCTIONS

COST OF SALE

LABOR RATE

PART NUMBERS

FORD USE ONLY-KEY PUNCH CHECK DIGIT

111063 | 7

111056 [0]

Model A Pickup

Ford

1930

FORD USE ONLY-KEY PUNCH CHECK DIGIT

STAPLE ATTACHMENTS HERE

SERVICE ADVISOR

LICENSE NO.   OWNER'S NAME   MODEL OR NAME

PROGRAM CODE   AUTHORIZATION

VEHICLE IDENTIFICATION (WARRANTY) NUMBER

PART NUMBERS

PREFIX   BASIC   SUFFIX   NAME   QTY.   EACH

PARTS

REPAIR

COST OF SALES - LABOR

TOTAL

FORD USE ONLY-KEY PUNCH CHECK DIGIT

111056 [0]

X   CUSTOMER'S SIGNATURE

(SIGNED)   DEALER GENERAL MANAGER OR AUTHORIZED PERSON   (DATE)

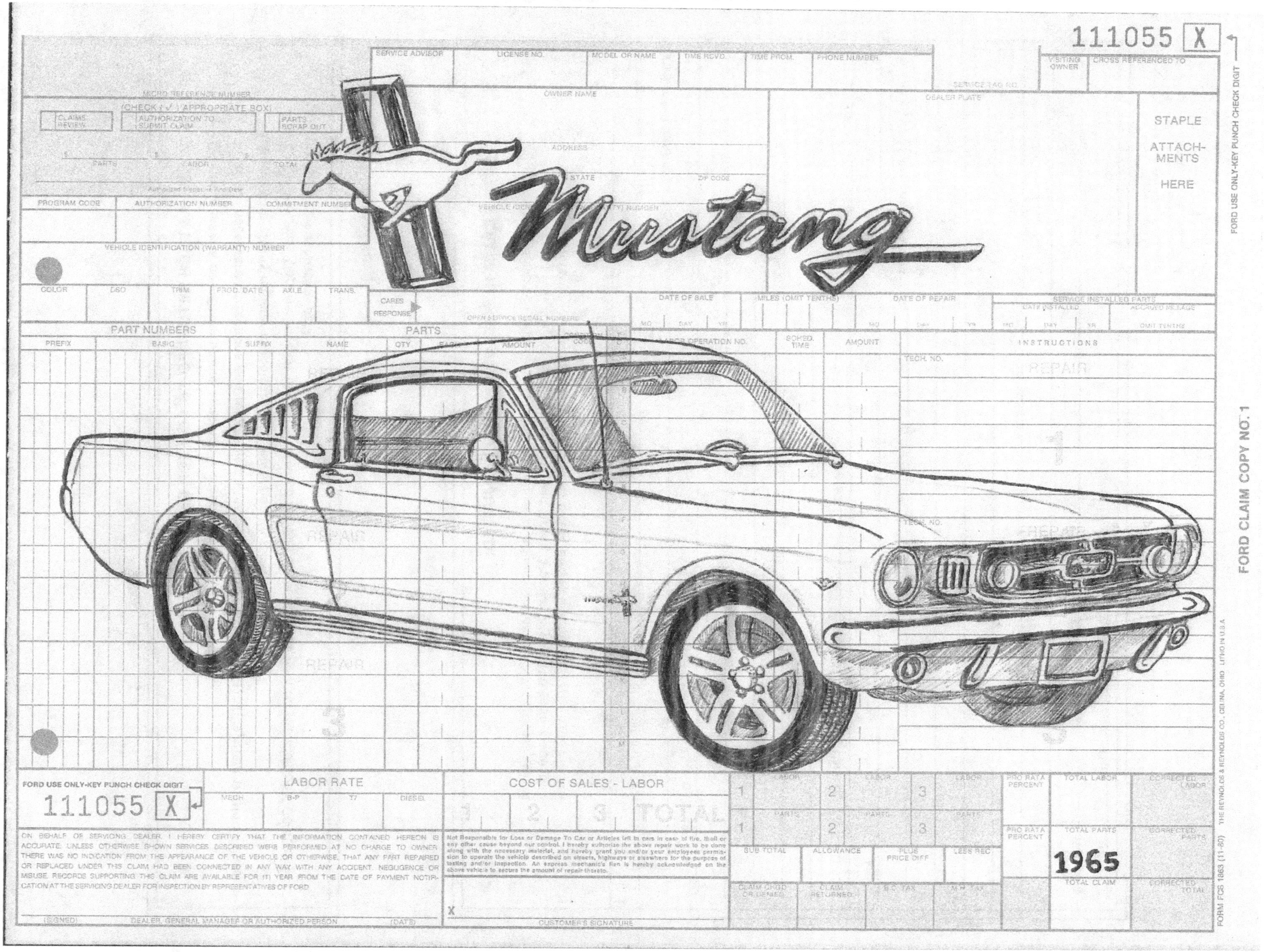
111055 X
FORD USE ONLY-KEY PUNCH CHECK DIGIT
Mustang
STAPLE
ATTACH-
MENTS
HERE
FORD CLAIM COPY NO. 1
PART NUMBERS
PARTS
LABOR RATE
COST OF SALES - LABOR
1965
TOTAL CLAIM

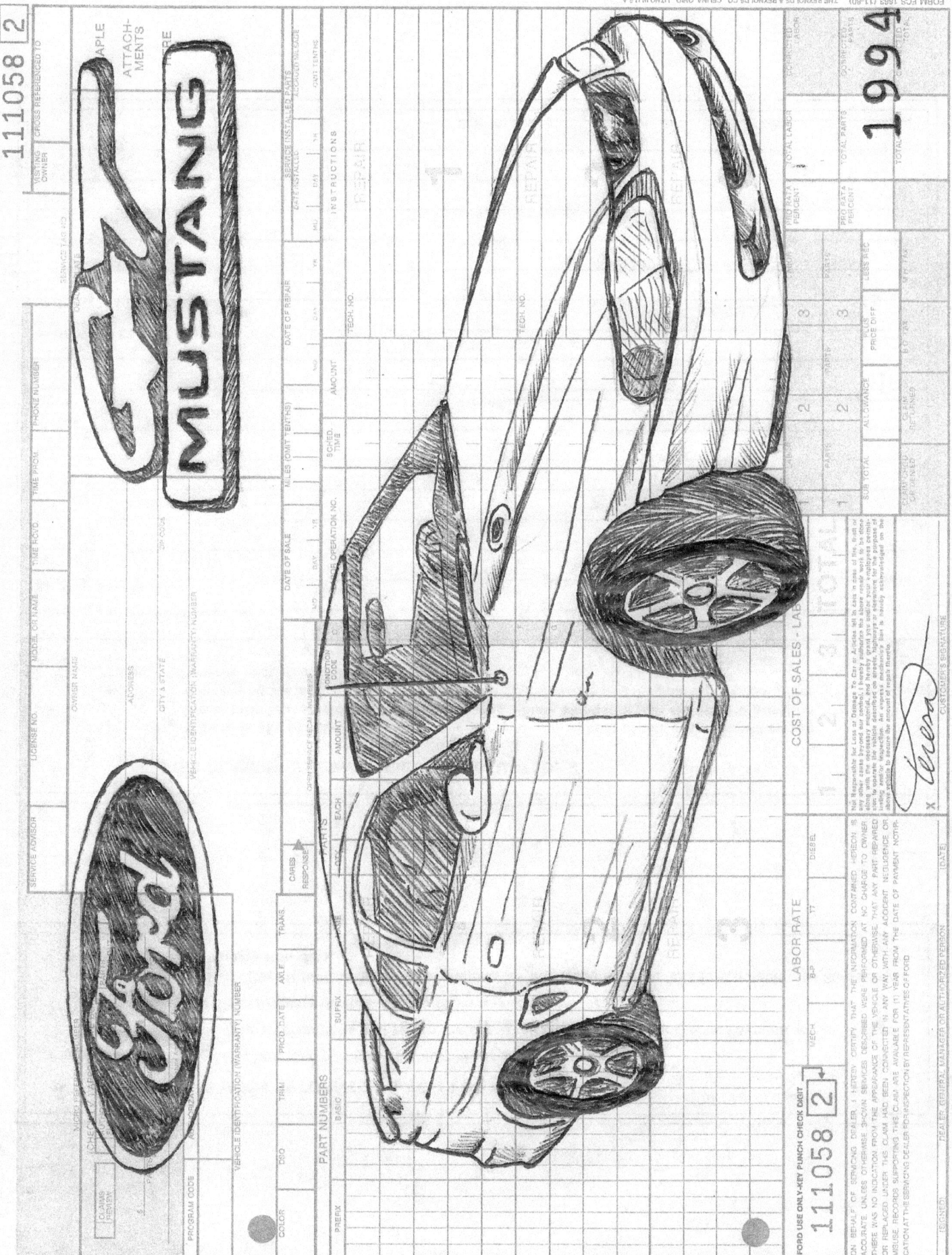

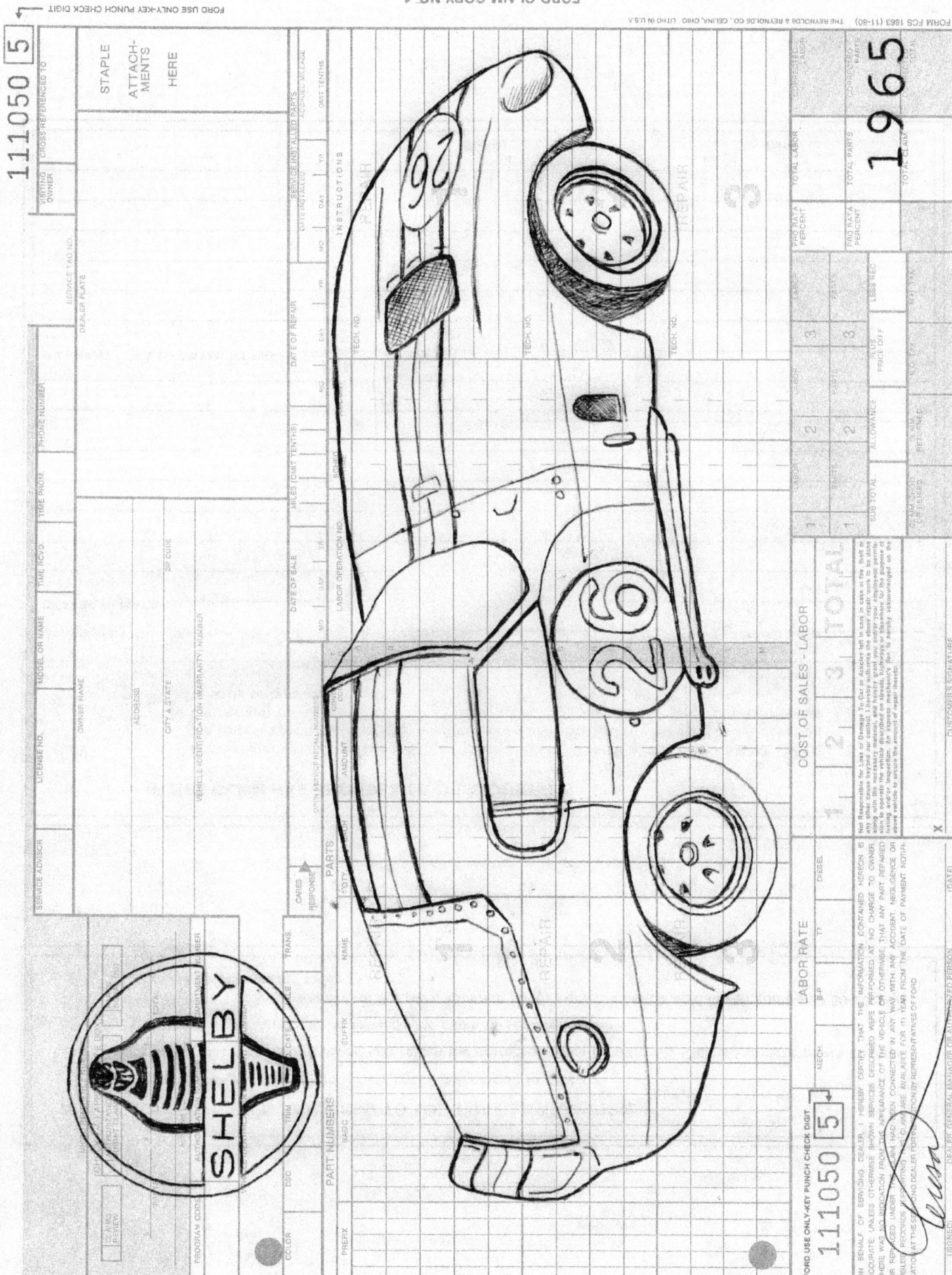

Thunderbird

1958

OREGON MYTBD

111062 6

COST OF SALES - LABOR

TOTAL

LABOR RATE